CW00450143

WORLD WAR ONE: 1914

Philip J. Haythornthwaite

Front cover illustration: The face of war – walking-wounded leave the firing-line during the German attack on Antwerp. The two British Royal Marines in the foreground wear infantry uniform (but gaiters instead of puttees), khaki having replaced their original blue uniform. The equipment is the standard 1908 web pattern, which had five cartridge-pouches at each side of the waist-belt, supported by shoulder-braces. Hanging by the bayonet-scabbard at the left side is the shaft of the entrenching-tool. The soldiers in dark greatcoats in the background are Belgians.

Back cover illustrations:
Top: German machine-gun crew, wearing greatcoats but with knapsacks removed to aid mobility. The standard weapon was the MG 1908 (*Maschinengewehr* 1908-pattern); the legs on its carriage were spread to allow it to be fired from the lowest possible position. Note the water-can and hose leading to the jacket of the barrel for cooling purposes. In the mid-ground is the section-commander and his NCO, and two runners sheltering behind a portable, bullet-proof observation-shield.

Bottom: Russian infantry wearing their service uniform: a light olive-khaki shirt (*Gimnastirka*) with cuffs fastened by a button, frontal opening and side pockets, worn outside the matching trousers, beneath the brown leather waist-belt with two frontal ammunition-pouches, a matching cap (sometimes with khaki leather peak) bearing an orange/white/black oval cockade, and unstained boots which were usually blackened. Detachable shoulder-straps were usually khaki on one side and facing-coloured on the other, bearing regimental identity and red rank-lace. The grey-brown greatcoat is worn bandolier-fashion. The firearm is the 1891 7.65mm rifle with bayonet kept permanently fixed.

1. The standing armies of all nations were supplemented by the calling to the colours of reservists of various kinds, and by encouraging mass enlistment: this is a typical group of British recruits, probably to the Royal Engineers, photographed in September 1914 at Gillingham, Kent. A caption on the original photograph states 'having a fine time . . .'

WORLD WAR ONE:
1914

Philip J. Haythornthwaite

ARMS AND
ARMOUR

▲2

2. Strangely, the commencement of hostilities was greeted with jubilation in certain quarters throughout Europe; here, Austrian officer-cadets salute their Emperor. All wear the standard soft peaked cap and greatcoat in pike-grey (*Hechtgrau*), though the officer

▼3

taking the salute wears the stiff-sided version of the kepi which was restricted to staff and general officers.

3. Departing for the front: French infantry march out of Paris to the cheers of the population. Among the least modern of the uniforms of the

combatant nations, the French infantry had a single-breasted blue tunic, but the rank-and-file wore a dark-blue double-breasted greatcoat, with red collar-patches bearing the regimental number in blue. The scarlet kepi had a blue band bearing the regimental number in red,

but for active service the red was concealed by the 1912-pattern blue-grey fabric cap-cover. The red (*garance*) trousers even at this early stage of the war were sometimes covered by blue-grey overalls.

INTRODUCTION

First published in Great Britain in 1989 by Arms and Armour Press, Artillery House, Artillery Row, London SW1P 1RT.

Distributed in the USA by Sterling Publishing Co. Inc., 2 Park Avenue, New York, NY 10016.

Distributed in Australia by Capricorn Link (Australia) Pty. Ltd., P.O. Box 665, Lane Cove, New South Wales 2066, Australia.

© Arms and Armour Press Limited, 1989
All rights reserved. No part of this book may be reproduced or transmitted in any form or by any means electronic or mechanical including photocopying recording or any information storage and retrieval system without permission in writing from the Publisher.

British Library Cataloguing in Publication Data:
Haythornthwaite, Philip J. (Philip John), 1951–
World War One: 1914. – (Soldiers Fotofax)
1. World War 1
I. Title II. Series
940.3
ISBN 0-85368-904-0

Designed and edited by DAG Publications Ltd.
Designed by David Gibbons; layout by Cilla Eurich; typeset by Ronset Typesetters Ltd, Darwen, Lancashire, and Typesetters (Birmingham) Ltd, Warley, West Midlands; camerawork by M&E Reproductions, North Fambridge, Essex; printed and bound in Great Britain by The Alden Press, Oxford.

When 'The Great War' broke out in the late summer of 1914, the concept of camouflaged uniform had not been accepted by some of the combatant nations, with the result that some troops sported styles of dress more attuned to the mid-19th century than to a 'modern' war. In matters of uniform, Britain was among the most advanced of all the European nations, having adopted a universl khaki serge 'service dress' as early as 1902, largely as a result of the lessons of the Boer War. Germany had introduced a uniform of field-grey in 1910, but retained the old spiked helmet (*Pickelhaube*), although with a camouflaged cover; other troops wore the shako, hussars the fur busby and the lancers the traditional *czapka*. From her experience in the Russo-Japanese War, Russia had evolved a light greenish-khaki service uniform by 1907; the Austrians introduced a pike-grey uniform in 1909, but their cavalry still retained their old coloured uniforms. Belgium was in course of a degree of uniform-modernization, but still retained the shako and cavalry uniforms which included *czapkas* and red trousers. Of all the major combatants in 1914, France's army wore the most out-dated uniform, for though one of the most powerful in the world and with considerable experience of colonial warfare, the military establishment had steadfastly resisted modernization. Experiments had been made to find a more practical service-dress, including a blue-beige uniform in 1906,a khaki uniform with felt helmet (*tenue réséda*) in 1910–12, and 'horizon blue' with leather or steel helmet in 1912, but none had been adopted and the army took the field in 1914 wearing blue coats with red kepi and trousers, and cuirassiers still wearing breastplates and maned helments, uniforms more suited to the 1850s. The more minor combatant nations were influenced by the styles of one or other of the major powers, but in the Balkan states of Serbia and Montenegro the issue of uniforms was not comprehensive and many of the combatants wore only scraps of issue uniform, or even entirely civilian clothing.

The illustrations here were almost all taken on active service in 1914, during the opening campaigns of the war; a few exceptions are included only because they illustrate the uniform-style especially well. Numerous illustrated periodicals were published at the time, though care should be taken when referring to these, as contemporary captions can be misleading; many of the photographs published as ostensible 'war' pictures in 1914 actually depict pre-war manoeuvres, including a famous example reputedly showing French vedettes searching for Germans, but actually photographed in 1911 and showing the experimental *tenue réséda*!

The series: it is the intention in this series of fotofax titles to cover each year of the first World War in contemporary photographs, and in the central data sections to enumerate the major patterns of uniform, personal equipment and weaponry of the combatant nations. Because of the peculiar nature of the campaigns of 1914 with the transition from peace to war establishment, the data section in the present title is concerned primarily with examples of organizational tables and sample orders-of-battle, and the various facing colours and uniform distinctions worn in the early months of the war; illustrations of weapons and personal equipment will appear in succeeding titles.

Philip J. Haythornthwaite

▲4 ▼5

▼6

4. French cuirassiers marching through Paris *en route* to the war; a British girl distributes packets of cigarettes. Amazingly archaic, these troopers wear the regulation dark-blue tunic (black for officers) with red facings, and red breeches with black stripes; they retain the iron cuirass with brass shoulder-scales and the maned helmet, though the latter was covered with fabric (of various shades) as a concession to active service.

5. The campaign uniform of the German Army in the first year of the war was the 1910-pattern field-grey (a lighter and less greenish shade than that worn later), with deep cuffs, coloured piping according to the branch of service and shoulder-straps bearing the regimental designation; greatcoat with coloured collar-patches, brown leather equipment and hide knapsack, and the spiked helmet or *Pickelhaube*. This is an infantry outpost in Belgium during the first advance.'

6. German infantry halted on the road near Brussels, with regimental transport in the background. The most distinctive item of German uniform, which became a symbol of German militarism, was the spiked helmet. Made of black leather, it had a brass spike and large brass plate (white-metal for some regiments) in the shape of the Imperial eagle, though regimental distinctions existed and some states displayed their own coats of arms. In the field the *Pickelhaube* had a field-grey cloth cover with regimental number on the front (originally red, green after August 1914), a number repeated in red on the field-grey shoulder-straps of the tunic. The unit illustrated is Regt. No. 36, 'von Blumenthal', from Magdeburg, part of IV Corps in 1914.

7. A German infantry band, apparently in the advance on Belgium, with army transport-wagons in the background. This is presumably a brigade or divisional band, assembled from the musicians of the component regiments, as a number of

different identities appear on the covers of the *Pickelhauben*. None wear the laced, projecting wings (*Waffenrock*) on the shoulders of the tunic which traditionally distinguished musicians.

8. The German Army laid great importance upon the machine-gun, and in addition to the machine-gun sections in each infantry regiment, special machine-gun units were formed. This infantry company is dug-in in a shallow trench in Belgium, the men's equipment being placed at the rear of the firing-line. Note the dragging-harness worn by three of the machine-gun crew; mounted on a four-legged sledge and weighing 140lb, the gun was carried by two men, one at each end of the sledge.

7▲

8▼

9. German machine-gun post in a hastily constructed defensive position, believed to be in the vicinity of Antwerp. The shoulder-strap numerals identify the unit as the Grenadier Regiment No. 12, 'Prinz Carl von Preussen' (2nd Brandenburg), a unit whose home district was Frankfurt and which in 1914 formed part of III Corps of von Kluck's First Army.

10. German artillerymen manhandling a field-gun into position in Belgium. This illustrates the design of the flaps on the rear skirts of the 1910-pattern *Waffenrock* (tunic); the artillery had red piping on the skirts and tunic front, but black piping on the collar and cuffs. Artillery helmets had a ball finial instead of a spike, which was obvious even when helmet-covers were worn, as here; compare with the spiked infantry helmet at extreme right. The greatcoat worn bandolier-style was a common practice. The wicker basket upon the gun-trail was a carrier for half a dozen shells, to enable the gun to open fire immediately.

▲9   ▼10

11▲

12▲   13▼

11. German hussars in Brussels, a scene which more resembles an earlier age. The fur busby or *colback* was worn on active service without its decorative cloth 'bag' and with a field-grey cover, with an oval cockade on the front of the style also worn on the shako. The field-grey hussar tunic or *Atila* had five field-grey braid loops across the breast and braid 'Austrian knots' at the point of the cuffs; the shoulder-straps were formed of two-colour braid, the regimental button colour (yellow or white) and the colour of the full-dress *Atila*. The officers in the foreground wear the busby without a cover, with the chinstrap fastened around the fur. Note the regimental standard in the background, and the laced belt of its bearer.

12. The British Army wore a universal uniform of khaki serge, introduced in 1902, the tunic having a turndown collar and patch pockets, with khaki trousers and puttees. Buttons were brass (allowed to tarnish on active service) and brass regimental titles were worn upon the shoulder-straps. The head-dress was a khaki cloth cap (worn here with khaki cover), bearing the regimental badge on the front, in this case that of the Royal Army Medical Corps; note also the Red Cross sleeve-badge. The equipment was normally of khaki-green webbing, but old leather equipment was not uncommon.

13. British officers' uniform resembled that of the rank-and-file, except for the design of the collar, and the patches on the cuffs, edged with khaki braid, bearing the rank insignia, in this case the single star of a second lieutenant; the lines of braid around the top of the cuff increased with rank. The brown leather belt was of the pattern known as 'Sam Browne', and could be worn with two shoulder-braces instead of the more common single brace. The cap and collar-badges illustrated (bronzed for service dress) are those of the Loyal Regiment (North Lancashire).

▲16

▲14 ▼15

14. A defensive position near Antwerp: British Royal Marines, wearing the khaki uniform which replaced the blue tunic and trousers and German-style 'Brodrick' cap worn by the Marines who had landed at Ostend. The Maxim gun in the foreground was used until the adoption of the Vickers machine-gun in 1915; although it was the infantry's main support weapon it existed in very small numbers when compared with the German Army: initially each infantry unit had only two Maxims. The position here is typical of those utilized in the early stages of the war, when the mobile nature of the fighting precluded the construction of extensive earthworks.

15. British cavalrymen passing through Termonde, south-west of Antwerp. The cavalry wore the same khaki 1902-pattern tunic as the infantry, but retained the 1903-pattern leather bandolier equipment abandoned by the infantry in favour of the 1908 web pattern. Visible here is the 1908-pattern cavalry sabre, carried at the left of the saddle, and note also the canvas bucket slung over the scabbard by the horseman at left. The Lee-Enfield magazine rifle was carried in a leather

'scabbard' at the right of the saddle, behind the rider's leg.

16. British sailors manning the defences of Antwerp. The British 'naval brigade' sent to Antwerp to assist the Belgians included bluejackets as well as Royal Marines; the former wore their blue naval uniform, landing rig including leather equipment, which in this photograph appears to resemble items of the 1888-pattern valise equipment, known as the 'Slade-Wallace'. Like the army, they were armed with the Lee-Enfield magazine rifle capable of a rate of fire of 15 rounds per minute in expert hands.

17. Not all the members of the British forces who landed on the continent in 1914 were officially enlisted; photographed on their return from Antwerp with two khaki-clad members of the Royal Marine Light Infantry, this group of the Brierfield Ambulance Corps (Lancashire) represent the civilian medical personnel who supplemented those of the services. This unit apparently served in the battle wearing their blue civilian uniform; 'It was like hell let loose,' one of them commented!

18. British cavalry watering their horses by a French river. In the modernization which followed the Boer War, from 1903 the lance was classified as a purely ceremonial weapon; but the 'lance lobby' was sufficiently influential to have it re-classified as a combatant weapon in 1909, and as such it was carried in 1914 (in common with the armies of many other European nations). Note the khaki neck-shades attached to the rear of the caps, worn in hot weather.

17▲

18▼

▲20

19. Many armies used bicycles for units of scouts. This British lance-corporal, receiving directions from a French civilian, wears the full 1908 web equipment (less the knapsack), with haversack and 1907-pattern bayonet at the left side; other equipment (including rifle and a chipped enamel mug) is lashed to the cycle. He wears the brass crossed-flags badge of a trained signaller on the left forearm, carries a binocular-case and has furled signal-flags tied to the cross-bar of the bicycle.

20. A British Maxim-gun section on the march, probably in the operations around Mons. Each British infantry unit had a Maxim section of two guns, served by an officer and twelve men, mostly expert marksmen. In addition to the Maxim itself, each gun was equipped with 3,500 rounds with a further 8,000 in reserve, necessitating the use of mule-transport. The men illustrated wear the 1908 web equipment, though the sergeant in command is also equipped with a pistol-holster, an item not normally carried by infantry NCOs.

▲19 ▼21

21. A British field-gun in action across a country lane, partly camouflaged by the hedgerows. The principal weapons of the mobile field artillery were the 13pdr and 18pdr guns, with ammunition carried in their limbers, one sited here to the right of the fieldpiece. The NCO at the rear is resting upon a swivelling bar which could be used as a seat. 13pdrs similar to this were the Royal Horse Artillery guns used in the immortal stand of 'L' Battery at Néry on 1 September 1914.

22. A British heavy gun at the moment of firing, showing the great recoil of the barrel. The moving barrel absorbed the recoil which otherwise would caused the gun to roll back many yards. The gunners in action here are in typical active-service dress, some wearing woollen cap-comforters, and all are protecting their ears from the blast.

23. The British Expeditionary Force was very rapidly in the front line; here a battalion breaks its march in a Belgian street, near Mons, rifles being stacked in the road and equipment piled alongside. This is apparently a unit of the Royal Welch Fusiliers (the shoulder-strap insignia consisting of a brass grenade over the letters 'R.W.F.'), both of whose regular battalions were in the BEF, the 1st Battalion in the 22nd Brigade (7th Division) and the 2nd Battalion in the 19th Brigade.

24. One of the most remarkable action photographs of the early stages of the war: transport-wagons of the 1st Battalion, The Middlesex Regiment under shrapnel-fire at Signy Signets, 8 September 1914, in which nine horses were killed and a water-cart riddled. As the infantrymen dive for cover, an officer (centre) is hit (there appears to be a gash on the right side of his head); he is probably a staff officer of the 19th Infantry Brigade, carrying binoculars and map-case and with automobile goggles around his cap. Remarkably, this photograph was published in 1914 despite its somewhat dispiriting content.

25. Scottish regiments wore similar equipment to the remainder of the British Army, but officially had tunics with rounded front skirts (as worn by the figure second left), and the kilt, hose, gaiters and glengarry cap of traditional Highland military dress. This group of lightly wounded prisoners (captured around Mons) wear the 'Government' (Black Watch) tartan kilt; the plain blue glengarry and red-and-black hose indicates the Black Watch, and the red-and-white hose and glengarry-band the Argyll and Sutherland Highlanders.

26 ▲

26. The first British Territorial unit to see action (at Messines on 31 October) was the London Scottish; this group was photographed at a French railway station a few days before. They wore the khaki 'Highland' tunic, kilts of 'Hodden grey', blue glengarry with white-metal badge, grey hose and khaki spats, and grey hair sporrans with two black tails. As a concession to active service the sporran-tails and glengarry-badges were removed on 29 October. The battalion's Mk I Lee-Enfields jammed easily, so at Messines they picked up Mark IIIs from casualties, and even used captured German rifles.

27. Belgian infantry on the march, wearing the 1913-pattern uniform unsuited for the war: a shako with oilskin cover and red pompom (green for light infantry), often with the regimental number painted on the front, a double-breasted, dark-blue greatcoat over or instead of the 1913-pattern tunic (*vareuse*) with nine brass buttons, blue-grey trousers and leather gaiters; the man fourth from the left is a corporal, distinguished by his single cuff-chevron. In the background is a civilian wagon commandeered as army transport.

29 ▲

28. Belgian infantry in the war-damaged streets of Termonde. This was the usual service uniform at the outset of the war; double-breasted dark-blue greatcoat, blue-grey trousers, leather gaiters and a German-style dark-blue cloth forage-cap with a red band, bearing the national Belgian cockade (black/yellow/red) on the front. The standard infantry weapon was the 1889-pattern Belgian 7.65 Mauser rifle.

29. A Belgian machine-gun post. The Belgian uniform being so unsuited for active service, it was quickly replaced by the 'Yser' uniform (named from its use by the troops fighting on the River Yser). The old shako was replaced by a blue or green soft kepi with arm-of-service piping (blue-grey for infantry), the 1913-pattern tunic by a single-breasted dark-blue or grey tunic with seven grey metal buttons and coloured piping on the cuffs, and the blue-grey trousers replaced by wine-red corduroy with blue puttees and ankle-boots, shortages being made up from French stocks.

30. A relic of a bygone age: a captured German officer (third from right) pays an old-style courtesy by saluting a Belgian colour-party on the roadside. The Belgian infantry (left) wear greatcoats and covered shakos; the man bearing the flag has a waterproof cape over his field equipment. The prisoners are escorted by a cavalryman wearing a caped greatcoat.

31. A Belgian Guide with a captured German cavalry horse. The two élite regiments of Guides cavalry wore the 1913-pattern double-breasted cavalry tunic in dark-green with crimson collar and piping, and crimson overalls with double yellow stripe; their green full-dress dolman with orange braid was rarely if every worn on active service. The Guides were the only ones to wear the black fur busby (*colback*), but like all other cavalry carried the lance; here, its pennon of red over yellow over black is furled.

32. Belgian Guides. The man in the foreground carries a wicker basket containing carrier-pigeons, which were used to communicate between Brussels and Antwerp. In addition to their sabres and lances, the troopers carry the 1889-pattern Belgian 7.65mm Mauser carbine.

33. A Belgian Guide surveys the rubble of Haelen, a bombarded town; he wears the 1913 cavalry tunic with light-coloured breeches and long gaiters. The goggles around the laced forage-cap suggest that he is crewing some form of motorized transport.

34. A Belgian *Chasseur à cheval* NCO reconnoitering, taking advantage of a convenient road-sign, the legend on which has been obscured to hinder the enemy. He wears the 1913-pattern, dark-blue cavalry tunic with red piping (yellow for the 1st Chasseurs), blue-grey trousers with red stripes (1st yellow), and the shako covered with oilskin. The 1889 Mauser carbine is suspended from a belt-clip; the sabre is carried on the saddle.

32▲ 33▼

34▼

▲35

35. Belgian infantry with a dog-drawn machine-gun. Dog-carts were used extensively by the Belgian Army in 1914, though few were as heavy as this wooden version; some were merely machine-guns mounted on spoked wheels with

▼36

pneumatic tyres, with the dogs harnessed to the trail. The practice was a militarization of the dog-drawn milk-carts used in Belgian towns, but although the British Army experimented with the scheme it was not adopted by other nations.

36. Belgian field artillery in action, showing the recoil of the gun barrel. The crew wears a mixture of uniform, all with the dark-blue 1913-pattern tunic with scarlet piping, blue-grey trousers with scarlet stripe and black leather equipment; some

wear the field cap while the men at left retain the fur *talpack* (a squat busby) used by the field and horse artillery.

37. A Belgian fort outside Liège replying to the German bombardment; the guns are

protected by temporary field-works utilizing gabions (baskets filled with earth) and wicker hurdles, as would have been used two centuries before. The gunners wear dark-blue greatcoats with the skirts fastened back, and blue-grey trousers; their shakos with oilskin covers identify them as members of the Fortress Artillery.

38. King Albert (in the gateway) watches a detachment of Belgian cyclists. Cyclists of the two Carabinier regiments wore a peaked field cap, green 1913-pattern tunic with yellow piping and blue-grey trousers, but the men seen here wear a mixture of uniform, including shakos, the German-style field cap and the squat kepi of the 'Yser' uniform, with greatcoats and infantry equipment; the two NCOs nearest the camera wear the cavalry tunic, laced forage-cap and apparently puttees. Note how several men have turned back their greatcoat-cuffs to reveal the lining.

37▲   38▼

▲39

39. Belgian Civic Guardsmen at Antwerp. The *Gardes Civiques*, a 'home-guard'-style defence force, was not recognized by the Germans as part of the Belgian Army; thus, before the occupation of Brussels the Civic Guard was marched to the town hall and there surrendered their weapons, so as not to be treated as guerrillas. Their overcoat was like that of the army, but the black bowler hat was distinctive.

40. French infantry halted by the roadside at Amiens: the men wear their black leather waist-belts with 1877-pattern ammunition-pouches, but have removed the 1893-pattern knapsack which has the mess-tin strapped on top. The stacked rifles are the 1886/93 pattern 8mm Lebel. It is interesting to note that some of these men have their trousers worn outside their leather gaiters, and turned-up at the ankle.

41. French infantry defending a shell-damaged building which is apparently next to a cemetery; a picture probably posed for the photographer, but showing the large amount of equipment carried on the soldier's back, including a spare pair of boots, one on each side of the knapsack. Especially evident is the tan fabric 1892-pattern haversack over the right shoulder, and the unmistakable narrow metal scabbard of the Lebel rifle.

▼41

▼40

42 ▲

42. Peace and war: a dusty column of French infantry on the march past grape-harvesters in Champagne. The front skirts of the long dark-blue French greatcoat were commonly fastened back to free the legs, a fashion adopted by these men; all wear the 1912-pattern blue-grey kepi-cover with the possible exception of the man at the extreme right front, probably a non commissioned officer.

43. French infantry on the march, with transport-mules carrying the battalion's machine-guns and ammunition. From the numerals visible on the red collar-patches of the greatcoats, it is possible to identify this unit as the 8th Line Regiment, which in 1914 formed part of the 4th Brigade of the 2nd Infantry Division of I Army Corps in Lanrezac's Fifth Army.

43 ▼

ORDER OF BATTLE: BRITISH EXPEDITIONARY FORCE, 1914

(Organization was not totally constant during the period from August to November 1914)

Headquarters: Commander-in-Chief, Field Marshal Sir John D. P. French

Chief of Staff: Lt.Gen. Sir A. J. Murray

Cavalry Division: Maj.Gen. E. H. Allenby

1st Cavalry Bde: 2nd and 5th Dragoon Guards, 11th Hussars

2nd Cavalry Bde: 4th Dragoon Guards, 9th Lancers, 18th Hussars

3rd Cavalry Bde: 4th Hussars, 5th & 16th Lancers

4th Cavalry Bde: Composite Regt., Household Cavalry; 6th Dragoon Guards, 3rd Hussars

Artillery: 'D', 'E', 'I' & 'L' Btys. Royal Horse Artillery

5th (Independent) Cavalry Bde: 2nd Dragoons, 12th Lancers, 20th Hussars, 'J' Bty. R.H.A.

I Corps: Lt.Gen. Sir Douglas Haig

1st Division:

1st (Guards) Bde: 1/Coldstream Gds., 1/Scots Gds., 1/Black Watch, 1/Royal Munster Fusiliers

2nd Inf. Bde: 2/Royal Sussex, 1/Loyal North Lancashire, 1/Northamptonshire, 2/King's Royal Rifle Corps

3rd Inf. Bde: 1/Queen's West Surrey, 2/South Wales Borderers, 1/Gloucestershire, 2/Welsh

Cavalry: 'C' Sqdn. 15th Hussars

Artillery: 25, 26, 39 & 48 Bdes. Royal Field Artillery; '26' Heavy Bty. Royal Garrison Artillery

2nd Division:

4th (Guards) Bde: 2/Grenadier Gds., 2/ & 3/Coldstream Gds., 1/Irish Gds.

5th Inf. Bde: 2/Worcestershire, 2/Oxford & Bucks. Light Infantry, 2/Highland Light Infantry, 2/Connaught Rangers

6th Inf. Bde: 1/King's (Liverpool), 2/South Staffordshire, 1/Royal Berkshire, 1/King's Royal Rifle Corps

Cavalry: 'B' Sqdn. 15th Hussars

Artillery: 34, 36, 41 & 44 Bdes. R.F.A.; '35' Bty. R.G.A.

II Corps: Lt.Gen. Sir J.M. Grierson (died 17 Aug.); thereafter Gen. Sir Horace Smith-Dorrien

3rd Division:

7th Inf. Bde: 3/Worcestershire, 2/South Lancashire, 1/Wiltshire, 2/Royal Irish Rifles

8th Inf. Bde: 2/Royal Scots, 2/Royal Irish, 4/Middlesex, 1/Gordon Highlanders

9th Inf. Bde: 1/Northumberland Fusiliers, 4/Royal Fusiliers, 1/Lincolnshire, 1/Royal Scots Fusiliers

Cavalry: 'A' Sqdn. 15th Hussars

Artillery: 23, 30, 40 & 42 Bdes. R.F.A.; '48' Bty. R.G.A.

5th Division:

13th Inf. Bde: 2/King's Own Scottish Borderers, 2/Duke of Wellington's, 1/Royal West Kent, 1/King's Own Yorkshire Light Infantry

14th Inf. Bde: 2/Suffolk, 1/East Surrey, 1/Duke of Cornwall's Light Infantry, 2/Manchester

15th Inf. Bde: 1/Norfolk, 1/Bedfordshire, 1/Cheshire, 1/Dorset

Cavalry: 'A' Sqdn. 19th Hussars

Artillery: 8, 15, 27 & 28 Bdes. R.F.A.; '108' Bty. R.G.A.

19th Inf. Bde. (formed 22 August): 2/Royal Welch Fusiliers, 1/Cameronians, 1/Middlesex, 2/Argyll & Sutherland Highlanders

Line-of-communication Btn: 1/Devonshire (to 8th Inf. Bde. September)

III Corps: Maj.Gen. W. P. Pulteney

4th Division:

10th Inf. Bde: 1/Royal Warwickshire, 2/Seaforth Highlanders, 1/Royal Irish Fusiliers, 2/Royal Dublin Fusiliers

11th Inf. Bde: 1/Somerset Light Infantry, 1/East Lancashire, 1/Hampshire, 1/Rifle Brigade

12th Inf. Bde: 1/King's Own Lancaster, 2/Lancashire Fusiliers, 2/Royal Inniskilling Fusiliers, 2/Essex

Cavalry: 'B' Sqdn. 19th Hussars

Artillery: 14, 29, 32 & 36 Bdes. R.F.A.; '31' Bty. R.G.A.

6th Division:

16th Inf. Bde: 1/Buffs, 1/Leicestershire, 1/King's Shropshire Light Infantry, 1/York & Lancaster

17th Inf. Bde: 1/Royal Fusiliers, 1/North Staffordshire, 1/Leinster, 3/Rifle Brigade

18th Inf. Bde: 1/West Yorkshire, 1/East Yorkshire, 2/Sherwood Foresters, 2/Durham Light Infantry

Cavalry: 'C' Sqdn: 19th Hussars

Artillery: 12, 24 & 38 Bdes. R.F.A.; '24' Bty. R.G.A.

IV Corps: Maj.Gen. Sir H.S. Rawlinson, Bt.

7th Division:

20th Inf. Bde: 1/Grenadier Gds., 1/Scots Gds., 2/Border, 2/Gordon Highlanders

21st Inf. Bde: 2/Bedfordshire, 2/Green Howards, 2/Royal Scots Fusiliers, 2/Wiltshire

22nd Inf. Bde: 2/Queen's Royal West Surrey, 2/Royal Warwickshire, 1/Royal Welch Fusiliers, 1/South Staffordshire

Cavalry: Northumberland Hussars

Artillery: 'C', 'F' & 'T' Btys. R.H.A.; 22 & 35 Bdes. R.F.A.; 3 Bde. R.G.A.

3rd Cavalry Division:

6th Cavalry Bde: 3rd Dragoon Guards, 1st Dragoons, 10th Hussars

7th Cavalry Bde: 1st & 2nd Life Guards, Royal Horse Guards

Artillery: 'K' Bty. R.H.A.

Indian Corps: Lt.Gen. Sir J. Willcocks

Lahore Division: Ferozepore Bde: 1/Connaught Rangers, 57th Rifles, 129th Rifles, 9th Bhopal Regiment

Jullundur Bde: 1/Manchester, 15th & 47th Sikhs, 59th Rifles

Sirhind Bde: 1/Highland Light Infantry, 1/1st & 1/4th Gurkhas, 125th Rifles

Cavalry: 15th Lancers (Cureton's Multanis)

Artillery, etc: 5, 11 & 18 Bdes. R.F.A.; '109' Bty. R.G.A.; 34th Sikh Pioneers

Meerut Division:

Dehra Dun Bde: 1/Seaforth Highlanders, 2/2nd & 1/9th Gurkhas, 6th Jat Light Infantry

Garhwal Bde: 2/Leicestershire, 2/3rd Gurkhas, 1/ & 2/ Garhwal Rifles

Bareilly Bde: 2/Black Watch, 2/8th Gurkhas, 41st Dogras, 58th Rifles

Cavalry: 4th Cavalry

Artillery: 4, 9 & 13 Bdes. R.F.A.; '110' Bty. R.G.A.

Secunderabad Cavalry Brigade:
7th Dragoon Guards, 20th Deccan & 30th Poona Horse,
Jodhpore Lancers, 'N' Bty. R.H.A.

ORDER OF BATTLE: GERMAN ARMY, WESTERN FRONT

Disposition of Corps at the start of the war was as follows:
First Army (von Kluck): II, III, IV, IX Corps; III, IV, IX Reserve
Corps
Second Army (von Bülow): Guard, VII, X Corps; Guard, VII, X
Reserve Corps
Third Army (von Hausen): XI, XII, XIX Saxon Corps; XII Saxon
Reserve Corps
Fourth Army (Albrecht of Württemberg): VIII, XVIII Corps; VIII,
XVIII Reserve Corps
Fifth Army (Crown Prince): V, VI, XIII, XXI Corps; V, VI Reserve
Corps
Sixth Army (Rupert of Bavaria): I Bavarian, II Bavarian, III
Bavarian Corps; I Bavarian Reserve Corps
Seventh Army (von Heeringen): XIV, XV Corps; XIV Reserve
Corps

There is insufficient space for a complete German order of
battle for the outset of the war; but the typical organization of a
German Army corps is provided by the following composition of
II Corps of von Kluck's First Army, a corps based originally in
Pomerania with headquarters at Stettin.

II Corps
3rd Division:
5th Inf. Bde: 2nd Grenadiers (King Frederick William IV, 1st
Pomeranian)
9th Colberg Grenadiers (Graf Gneisenau, 2nd Pomeranian)
54th Infantry (von der Goltz, 7th Pomeranian)
6th Inf. Bde: 34th Fusiliers (Queen Victoria of Sweden)
42nd Infantry (Prince Moritz of Anhalt-Dessau, 5th
Pomeranian)
3rd Cavalry Bde: 2nd Queen's Cuirassiers (Pomeranian)
9th Uhlans (2nd Pomeranian)
3rd Field Artillery Bde: 2nd Field Artillery (1st Pomeranian)
38th Field Artillery (Upper Pomeranian)

4th Division:
7th Inf. Bde: 14th Infantry (Graf Schwerin, 3rd Pomeranian)
149th Infantry (6th West Prussian)
8th Inf. Bde: 49th Infantry (6th Pomeranian)
140th Infantry (4th West Prussian)
4th Cavalry Bde: 3rd Neumark Dragoons (von Derfflinger's
Horse Grenadiers)
12th Dragoons (von Arnim's, 2nd Brandenburg)
4th Field Artillery Bde: 17th Field Artillery (2nd Pomeranian)
53rd Field Artillery (Lower Pomeranian)

Supporting Troops: 2nd Foot Artillery (von Hindersin's), 15th
Foot Artillery (2nd West Prussian), 2nd (Pomeranian)
Pioneers and 2nd Pomeranian Train Battalion.

CHRONOLOGY: 1914

Western Front
3–27 August: German offensive extending from Belgium south
to Alsace, intent on rolling through Belgium, driving a wedge
between the Belgians and the newly arrived British Expeditionary Force in the north and the French in the south, then
wheeling south to capture Paris. Belgium largely overrun by
20 August, the B.E.F. forced to make a fighting retreat from
Mons (23 August), and at the Battle of Le Cateau (25–27
August). Initial French offensive plan was unrealistic and their
advances were repulsed by the Germans; French commanding
general, Joffre, forced to reorganize hurriedly.
5–10 September: Battle of the Marne. German attempt to
capture Paris halted by French Army in desperate fighting;
tactically indecisive, it was a huge strategic success for the
Allies which prevented an almost immediate German victory.
15 September–24 November: 'The Race to the Sea'. Both sides
attempted to outflank the other to the north, ever progressing
towards the North Sea coastline. BEF almost annihilated in
the First Battle of Ypres attempting to stop the German drive,
but successfully prevented the German capture of the Channel
ports.
14–24 December: Allied offensive repelled by German fixed
positions; the era of fluid manoeuvre ended, and static trench
warfare began. In the campaigning on the Western Front the
Allies had suffered almost a million casualties, and the
Germans almost as many.

Eastern Front
17 August–14 September: Russian invasion of East Prussia
conducted incompetently, defeated by the Germans at Tan-
nenberg (26–31 August) and First Battle of the Masurian
Lakes (9–14 September), defeats from which Russia never
fully recovered.
29 July–15 December: Austrian invasion of Serbia pushed on in
face of severe resistance to capture Belgrade (2 December);
Serbian counter-attack at Battle of Kolubra (3–9 December)
repelled the Austrian advance and recaptured Belgrade (15
December).
23 August–3 September: Austrian invasion of Russian Poland
driven back by Russians, Austrians being defeated decisively
at Rava Ruska (3–11 September).
17 September–2 November: German assistance to Austrians in
Galicia halted Russian advance, ending in the Battle of Lódź
(11–25 November), tactically a Russian victory but stra-
tegically an Austro-German success, preventing the Russians
from renewing the offensive. Stalemate on the Eastern Front
at the end of the year.

Turkish Front
29 October: Turkey joined the Central Powers by declaring war
against the Allies; Turkish offensive against the Russian
Caucasus halted at the Battle of Sarikamish (29 December).
Britain declared a protectorate over Egypt (18 December) to
defend the Suez Canal and began an invasion of Meso-
potamia (23 October); Basra captured from Turks (23
November).

Colonial Fronts
Operations against German bases in Africa, German East Africa
being defended stoutly. Several German island colonies captured, most notably Samoa, by British and Empire forces. Japan
entered the war on Allied side (23 August) and captured
Tsingtao, the German colony on the Chinese coast (7 November).

ORGANIZATIONAL TABLES: GERMAN ARMY, 1914

Although each army organized its forces in its own national methods, a number of similarities existed, in that it was usual for an Army Corps to be a completely self-contained entity with all necessary supporting services attached to the Corps, rather than to a central depot from which the necessary support units were drawn as required.

The following tables are typical, demonstrating the usual organization of the German Army in 1914, after mobilization. The most significant change between the pre-war and mobil-ization organization of a German Corps was that it was usual for the cavalry brigades to be withdrawn from the divisional organization and formed into independent Cavalry Divisions, leaving only a small cavalry contingent attached at infantry divisional level as a reconnaissance force. (The Order-of-Battle of II Corps above includes the pre-war disposition of cavalry with the infantry divisions).

A typical Army Corps upon mobilization was organized as follows:

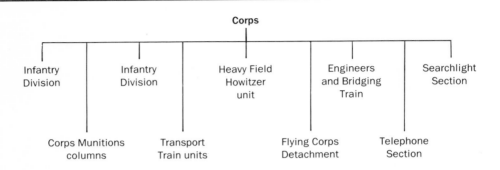

Divisional establishment in 1914 was:

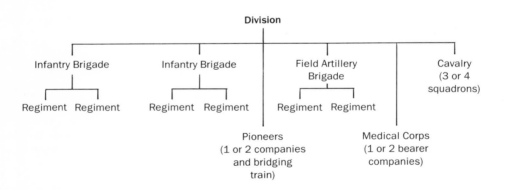

An infantry regiment in 1914 was organized in three battalions, with companies numbered consecutively from 1 to 12, with the separate machine-gun company (not attached to a battalion) numbered 13:

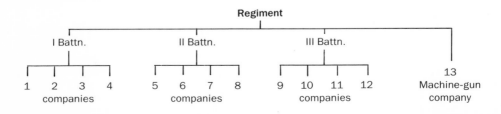

When the Cavalry Divisions were formed upon mobilization by withdrawing most of the divisional cavalry from their pre-war formations, the following was the typical cavalry organization:

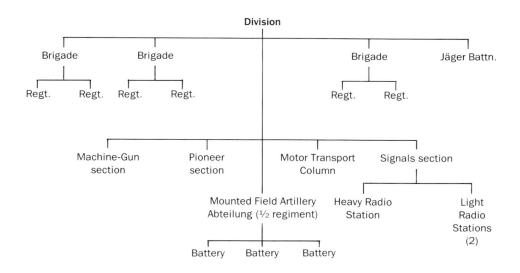

Artillery was divided into the Field Regiments, which manned the lighter guns attached at divisional level, and grouped in brigades; and the Foot Artillery Regiments, which manned the heavier guns attached at Corps level, normally allocated at one regiment per Army Corps. Field Regiments consisted of two *Abteilungen*, each of three batteries of six guns each, the batteries numbered consecutively throughout the regiment, from 1 to 6. The normal weapons of a regiment's 36 gun-crews were 7.7cm guns, but a number of IInd *Abteilungen* were armed with 10.5cm light field howitzers, so that two *Abteilungen* of howitzers were contained in each Army Corps. From October 1914 smaller batteries became common, each of four guns instead of six (thus increasing the number of batteries available while keeping the same total of guns), but 4-gun batteries did not become standard until 1915. Regimental organization of Field Artillery in 1914 was:

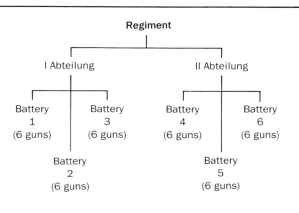

(For more extensive organizational details, see D. B. Nash's *Imperial German Army Handbook* as noted in bibliography).

DRESS DISTINCTIONS: BELGIAN ARMY, 1914

The following basic uniform-colours were worn by the Belgian Army at the outbreak of war:

Unit	Head-dress	Tunic	Trousers
Generals	kepi	dark-blue piped crimson	dark-blue, dark-blue stripe
Staff	kepi	green piped crimson	green piped-crimson
Infantry	shako	dark-blue piped blue-grey on 1913 uniform; otherwise piped red	blue-grey piped black
Grenadiers	bearskin cap	dark-blue piped scarlet	dark-blue, scarlet stripe
Chasseurs à Pied	shako	green piped yellow	blue-grey piped green
Carabiniers	Tyrolean hat	green piped yellow	blue-grey piped yellow
Carabinier Cyclists	kepi	green piped yellow	blue-grey piped yellow
Guides	colback (busby)	green piped crimson	crimson piped green
1st Lancers	czapka	dark-blue piped crimson	blue-grey piped crimson
2nd Lancers	czapka	dark-blue piped crimson	blue-grey piped crimson
3rd/5th Lancers	czapka	dark-blue piped white	blue-grey piped white

GERMAN CUFF PATTERNS

Designs of German cuff used
on the *Waffenrock*:
A: 'Brandenburg'
B: 'Swedish'
C: 'Saxon' or 'German'
D: 'French', with the *Litzen*
(lace loops) which
distinguished Guard units.

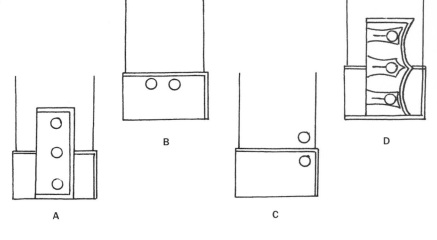

B

A

C

D

GERMAN HEADDRESS

Below: The *Pickelhaube*, worn here without its customary fabric cover, revealing the standard 'eagle' plate, metal fittings and cockades behind the chinscale-boss. Reputedly the first German to cross the Marne, this infantryman wears the greatcoat collar-patches, which were later discontinued.

Below: The German lancer *czapka* worn here with its service-dress field-grey cloth cover. This trooper — reputedly the German who approached England most nearly during the operations around Ostend — wears the dress tunic (*Uhlanka*) with epaulettes, though on campaign a field-grey version with pointed cuffs was worn. Excluding the Bavarian *Uhlans*, all cavalry wore standing collars.

Unit	Head-dress	Tunic	Trousers
4th Lancers	czapka	dark-blue piped blue	blue-grey piped blue
1st Chasseurs à Cheval	shako	dark-blue piped yellow	blue-grey piped yellow
2nd Chasseurs à Cheval	shako	dark-blue piped scarlet	blue-grey piped scarlet
4th Chasseurs à Cheval	shako	dark-blue piped scarlet	blue-grey piped scarlet
Field/Horse Artillery	talpack	dark-blue piped scarlet	blue-grey, scarlet stripes
Fortress Artillery	shako	dark-blue piped scarlet	blue-grey, scarlet stripes
Engineers	shako	dark-blue piped scarlet	blue-grey, scarlet stripes
Train	shako	dark-blue piped light-blue	blue-grey piped light-blue
Administration	kepi	dark-blue piped light-blue	blue-grey piped light-blue
Gendarmerie	bearskin cap	dark-blue piped scarlet	blue-grey
Medical Corps	kepi	dark-blue piped crimson	black, crimson stripe

DRESS DISTINCTIONS: FRENCH ARMY, 1914

The following basic uniform-distinctions were worn by the French Army at the outbreak of war:

Unit	Head-dress	Tunic	Buttons	Collar-patch	Trousers
Generals	kepi	black	yellow	—	scarlet, black stripe
Infantry	kepi, regtl. number	blue, faced red	yellow	red with blue regtl. number (white for territorials)	red, black stripe
Alpine Infantry	beret with grenade badge	blue, faced red	yellow	red with blue regtl. number	red, black stripe
Chasseurs à Pied	kepi with battn. number	blue	white	blue with yellow battn. number	blue-grey. yellow stripe
Alpine Chasseurs	beret with horn badge	blue	white	blue with yellow battn. number	blue-grey, yellow stripe
Cuirassiers	helmet	blue, faced red	yellow	blue with regtl. number	red, black stripe
Dragoons	helmet	blue, faced white	white	blue with red regtl. number	red, light-blue stripe
Chasseurs à Cheval	shako with horn badge	light-blue, faced crimson	white	crimson with light-blue regtl. number	red, light-blue stripe
Hussars	shako with knot-decoration (or helmet with horn badge)	light-blue	white	light-blue with red regtl. number	red, light-blue stripe
Artillery	kepi with regtl. number	blue, faced scarlet	yellow	scarlet with regtl. number	blue, scarlet stripe
Alpine Artillery	beret with grenade badge	blue, faced scarlet	yellow	scarlet with regtl. number	blue, scarlet stripe
Engineers	kepi with helmet-and-cuirass badge	blue, faced black	yellow	black with scarlet number	blue, scarlet stripe
Train	kepi with Corps number	light-blue, faced crimson	white	crimson with grey-blue number	crimson with grey-blue stripe

DRESS DISTINCTIONS: GERMAN ARMY, 1914

The following were the uniform-distinctions of the German Army, according to the 1910 regulations (worn until the introduction of the 1915 uniform). There is insufficient space to detail the considerable number of regimental variations and badge-designs; in the following table, 'R' indicates the use of a regimental distinctive- or facing-colour. All wore the standard tunic (*Waffenrock*) with stand-and-fall collar, with the exceptions that the Hussars wore the braided *Atila* and the *Uhlans* (lancers) the *Ulanka* tunic; all cavalry had standing collars save the Bavarian *Uhlans* and *Chevaux-légers*. Cuff-designs are indicated below by the letters 'S' (Swedish), 'B' (Brandenburg), 'Sx' (Saxon or 'German'), 'F' (French) and 'P' (pointed), in accordance with the line illustrations. Tunic-colour is abbreviated as 'F/G' (*Feldgrau* or 'field-grey') or 'G/G' (grey-green). The term *Pickelhaube* is used for artillery helmets below, even though they had a ball-top instead of a spike.

Unit	Head-dress	Cap-band & piping	Tunic
Generals	pickelhaube	red, piped red	F/G, S
General staff	pickelhaube	crimson, piped crimson	F/G, S
Staff officers	pickelhaube	crimson, piped crimson	F/G, S
Foot Guard regts. 1–4	pickelhaube	red, piped red	F/G, S
Foot Guard regt. 5	pickelhaube	red, piped red	F/G, B
Guard Grenadiers	pickelhaube	red, piped red	F/G, B
Infantry	pickelhaube	red, piped red	F/G, B
Infantry Leib. Regt.	pickelhaube	red, piped red	F/G, B
Guard Rifles	shako	black, piped light-green	G/G, F
Jägers	shako	light-green, piped light-green	G/G, S

Unit	Head-dress	Cap-band & piping	Tunic
Machine-Gun Btns.	shako	red, piped red	G/G, S
2nd Guard Machine-Gun Btn.	shako	black, piped red	G/G, F
Field Artillery	pickelhaube	black, piped red	F/G, S
Foot Artillery	pickelhaube	black, piped red	F/G, B
Cuirassiers	metal helmet	R, piped R	F/G, S
Dragoons	pickelhaube	R, piped R	F/G, S
Hussars	colback	R, piped R	F/G, S
Uhlans	czapka	R, piped R	F/G, P
Mounted Jäger regts. 1–7	metal helmet	light-green, piped light-green	G/G, S
Mounted Jäger regts. 8–13	pickelhaube (officers, metal helmet)	light-green, piped light-green	G/G, S
Pioneers	pickelhaube	black, piped red	F/G, S
Railway Battns.	pickelhaube	black, piped red	F/G, S
Airship Battns.	shako	black, piped red	F/G, S
Signal Battns.	shako	black, piped red	F/G, S
Aviation Battns.	shako	black, piped red	F/G, S
Motor Transport Battns.	peaked cap	black, piped red	F/G, S
Train	peaked cap	light-blue, piped light-blue	F/G, S
Medical Corps	peaked cap	blue, piped red	F/G, S
Veterinary Corps	peaked cap	black, piped crimson	F/G, S
Ordnance Corps	peaked cap	black, piped red	F/G, B
Fortification personnel	peaked cap	black, piped red	F/G, S
Military officials	peaked cap	blue, piped white	F/G, S
Bavarian infantry	pickelhaube	red, piped red	F/G, B
Bavarian Jägers	shako	light-green, piped light-green	F/G, S
Bavarian Machine-Gun Btns.	shako	light-green, piped light-green	F/G, S
Bavarian heavy cavalry	pickelhaube	red, piped red	F/G, S
Bavarian Chevaux-légers	pickelhaube	R, piped R	F/G, S
Saxon infantry	pickelhaube	red, piped red	F/G, Sx
100th/101st Grenadiers	pickelhaube	red, piped red	F/G, S
108th Saxon Rifles	shako	black, piped light-green	G/G, Sx
Saxon heavy cavalry	metal helmet	R, piped R	F/G, S
Saxon Foot Artillery	pickelhaube	black, piped red	F/G, Sx
Saxon Train	peaked cap	—	F/G, Sx
Württemberg infantry	pickelhaube	red, piped red	F/G, B
119th/123rd Grenadiers	pickelhaube	red, piped red	F/G, S
Hessian infantry	pickelhaube	red, piped red	F/G, B
109th Grenadiers	pickelhaube	red, piped red	F/G, S
Mecklenburg infantry	pickelhaube	red, piped red	F/G, B
Mecklenburg-Schwerin military officials	peaked cap	blue, piped white	F/G, B

Shoulder-straps were different for each regiment; of the uniform-colour, they bore the regimental number or distinctive badge, and coloured piping. The piping was arranged in the following scheme:

Guard regiments: colours white, red, yellow, light-blue and white for 1st–5th regiments respectively. Others had piping according to the Army Corps:

white:	Corps I, II, IX, X, XII, I Bavarian
red:	III, IV, XI, XIII, XV, XIX, II Bavarian
yellow:	V, VI, XVI, XVII, III Bavarian
light-blue:	VII, VIII, XVIII, XX
light-green:	XXI

XIV Corps had variously coloured distinctions. Other colours were:

Jäger and Rifles:	light-green piping
Cavalry:	regimental colouring
Foot Artillery:	white piping
Railway, Airship, Aviation and Motor Transport Battns.:	light-grey piping
Pioneers, Signals:	black shoulder-straps piped red
Train:	light-blue straps piped light-blue
Medical officers:	red piping
Medical orderlies:	dark-blue straps piped light-blue
Stretcher-bearers:	crimson straps
Veterinary personnel and military officials:	crimson piping
Fortification officers:	red/black piping

(For more extensive uniform details, see A. Mollo's *Army Uniforms of World War I* as noted in bibliography).

SOURCES AND BIBLIOGRAPHY

Among the enormous amount of literature concerning the First World War, the following are among the most useful for the events and armies of the first months of the war:

Ascoli, D. *The Mons Star: The British Expeditionary Force, 1914* (London, 1981).

Brown, M., and Seaton, S. *The Christmas Truce* (London, 1984).

Carew, T. *The Vanished Army* (London, 1964).

Craster, J.M. *Fifteen Rounds a Minute* (London, 1976).

French of Ypres, Viscount. *1914* (London, 1919).

Hammerton, Sir J. (ed.) *The Great War: 'I Was There'* vol. I (London, n.d.).

Hicks, J.E. *French Military Weapons* (New Milford, Connecticut, 1964).

——. *German Weapons, Uniforms, Insignia* (Le Canada, California, 4th ed. 1963).

Macdonald, L. *1914* (London, 1987).

Mollo, A. *Army Uniforms of World War I* (Poole, 1977).

Nash, D.B. *German Infantry 1914–18* (London, 1971).

——. *Imperial German Army Handbook 1914–18* (London, 1980).

Owen, E. *1914, Glory Departing* (London, 1986).

Tuchman, B.W. *August 1914* (London, 1962).

A wide range of photographs can be found in many contemporary periodicals: for example, *The Graphic; The Great War* (ed. H.W. Wilson and J.A. Hammerton, London 1914); *Illustrated London News; Illustrated War News; Navy & Army Illustrated; The Times History of the War; The War Budget,* etc.

GERMAN STATE COCKADES

German state colours were worn on the left cockade on the helmet (behind the chinscale-boss), with the national (*Reich*) red/white/black cockade on the right side. On the field cap, the state cockade was carried below the *Reich* cockade. Units wearing shakos (except Saxon), colbacks and czapkas had oval cockades which might vary from the ordinary pattern. Colours were as follows.

Prussia:	black/white/black; oval cockade, white/black
Bavaria:	white/light-blue/white; oval cockade, white/light-blue
Saxony:	green/white/green; oval cockade, white/green
Württemberg:	black/red/black; oval cockade, black/red
Hessen:	white/red/white
Mecklenburg:	blue/yellow/red; oval cockade, white/blue/red, trimmed with yellow braid
Baden:	yellow/red/yellow; oval cockade, yellow/red
Oldenburg:	blue/red/blue
Brunswick:	blue/yellow/blue
Anhalt:	green
Saxe-Weimar:	green/yellow/black
Saxe-Coburg, Meiningen and Altenburg:	green/white/green
Schwarzburg-Rudolstadt:	blue/white/blue
Schwarzburg-Sonderhausen:	white/blue/white
Waldeck-Reuss:	yellow/black/red
Lippe:	yellow/red
Schaumburg-Lippe:	white/red/blue
Bremen:	white/red/white
Hamburg:	white with red Iron Cross
Lübeck:	white with red Maltese Cross

44. The French Army's principal machine-guns in the early 20th century were variations on the Hotchkiss gun, the 1900- and 1914-patterns of Hotchkiss and the 1907-pattern St-Etienne; all had spindly legs and a seat for the gunner, and all except the 1914 Hotchkiss had a wheel at the left side for elevation.

▲45

45. A French infantryman
samples English Christmas
pudding in December 1914. He
wears the grey-blue kepi-cover,
and his greatcoat bears diagonal
rank-bars, probably in the
metallic lace which indicated a
sergeant. The 1893-pattern
black leather knapsack has the
▼47

1852-pattern mess-tin strapped
on top.

46. French dragoons wore the
crested helmet with fabric
cover, dark-blue tunic with
white facings and red trousers
with sky-blue stripes. Here a
dragoon officer (on foot)

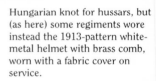

▲46

converses with a light
cavalryman whose sky-blue
tunic appears to bear the
crimson collar-patches and
white trefoil epaulettes of the
chasseurs à cheval. Light
regiments wore a sky-blue
shako bearing a brass horn
badge for chasseurs and a

Hungarian knot for hussars, but
(as here) some regiments wore
instead the 1913-pattern white-
metal helmet with brass comb,
worn with a fabric cover on
service.

47. French artillery firing at the Steinbach heights. These 120mm guns of the 1877 'Système de Bange' were too heavy for mobile field use, but were used for more static positions. The names painted on the barrels include 'Kultur', the Allies' ironic term for the uncivilized German behaviour as protrayed in Allied propaganda. The gunners here wear grimy fatigue uniform; the artillery kepi was blue with red piping and numeral, and the trousers blue with red stripe.

48. The *Chasseurs Alpins* (Alpine Chasseurs), alias 'Blue Devils', were among the most renowned units of the French Army. Highly trained for operating in mountainous terrain, they carried infantry equipment plus an alpenstock, and wore a dark-blue tunic and puttees, white trousers, and, most characteristically, a dark-blue beret which on campaign would have a white cover. These Chasseurs are crewing a light mountain howitzer.

49. The Belgian defenders of Nieuport were supported by French units; here a French medical officer attends to a casualty in the trenches. The doctor wears the black tunic of French officers, and has the red top of his kepi concealed by a cover. The facing-colour of the medical personnel was crimson, and their ordinary *garance* trousers had a wide black stripe for officers.

50. The most colourful of the French infantry, the Zouaves were Frenchmen dressed in North African style. Their uniform was highly impractical: red cap (*chéchia*), blue waistcoat and bolero-style jacket with red braid, and voluminous red trousers. This was modified progressively in the first months of the war, the white service-dress trousers being replaced by khaki and the caps issued with a blue cover. Eventually these impractical garments were replaced by 'mustard'-coloured uniforms, but in the early part of the war the classic zouave uniform illustrated was retained.

48 ▲　　49 ▼

50 ▼

51. Among the troops recruited by the French Army in North Africa were the Algerian *Tirailleurs*, commonly known as 'Turcos', who continued to wear their African uniform; this group was photographed during a halt on the march near Rheims. Their original sky-blue zouave uniform with voluminous white trousers was eventually replaced by a more practical sky-blue greatcoat and khaki trousers and tunic (*vareuse*) at about the turn of 1914/15, and the zouave caps equipped with a sky-blue cover; ultimately they adopted a uniform of 'mustard'-khaki.

52. The Senegalese *Tirailleurs* of the French Army wore zouave-style head-dress and blue tunic and trousers, but even before the outbreak of war were issued with a khaki uniform and cap-cover, the tunic (*paletot*) having extremely short skirts; this adumbrated the adoption of mustard-coloured uniforms by all French colonial units in 1915.

▲51 ▼52

53. Senegalese *Tirailleurs* of the French Army man a defence-line at Pervyse, between Dixmude and Nieuport, wearing their *chéchia* head-dress and greatcoats of infantry pattern (issued for service in the European climate). It was stated in 1914 that the African complexion of the Senegalese assisted in camouflaging them!

54. French 'marines' (naval infantry) were deployed on land during the early months of the war, serving at Ypres and Dixmude, for example. They carried equipment like that of the infantry, with the greatcoat, but retained the blue cap with pompom which traditionally distinguished French 'bluejackets'. The boy scout at the head of column in this photograph is acting as a guide while the unit passes through his town.

55. This group of Austrian staff officers (with German attaché, right) illustrates the staff version of the Austrian uniform introduced in 1909, a pike-grey single-breasted tunic, breeches with red stripes (for generals) and black riding-boots or brown leather gaiters. The pike-grey kepi in this 'stiff' form was worn only by staff officers and thus was nicknamed the 'artificial brain'! General officers' rank was indicated by one to three silver stars on the scarlet collar-patch, which had gold zigzag lace edging. Leatherwork was brown.

53 ▲   54 ▼

55 ▼

56. Austrian artillery in Brussels: Austrian heavy guns assisted the Germans in Belgium. This illustrates excellently the 1909-pattern pike-grey uniform worn by all except cavalry, a single-breasted tunic with patch pockets and facing-coloured collar-patches (scarlet for artillery) and pike-grey kepi with leather peak and circular badge bearing the imperial cipher (FJI) in the centre. Officers carried swords and automatic pistols.

▲56 ▼57

57. Austrian dragoons on the march, wearing the 1905-pattern leather dragoon helmet with brass edging and eagle-plate; on active service they were more usually covered with grey linen or were painted grey. The cavalry tunic was light-blue with madder-red facings, worn with madder-red breeches and brown leather equipment; the fur-lined light-blue over-jacket (*Pelz*) is not visible. Arms were the 1869-pattern cavalry sabre with steel hilt, and the 1890 Steyer-Mannlicher 8mm carbine.

58. The Crown Prince visiting Austrian troops in Poland; the men wear the pike-grey greatcoat with pointed collar-patch (*Paroli*) in the facing-colour, and the soft pike-grey kepi and brown leather equipment; officers have fur collars. Of especial note is the continuing use of the *Feldzeichen*, the green sprig worn on the head-dress, a relic of the 'field-sign' of the 17th century, which continued to be worn by the Austrian Army into the mid-20th century.

▼58

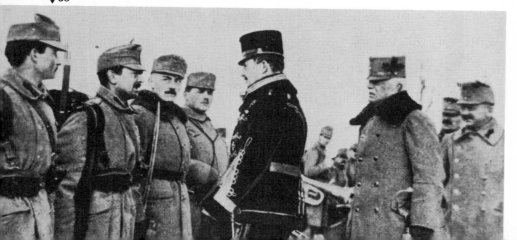

59. An Austrian siege-howitzer in action in Galicia. For campaign in winter the gunners wear greatcoats and a variety of over-shoe gaiters, with the soft cloth kepi (which had a front flap fastening with two buttons) and goggles. Shorter coats with fur collars are also in evidence.

60. Austrian prisoners with Serbian guards. The Austrians wear the pike-grey 1909-pattern tunic and trousers, the two nearest the camera with the three white stars on the collar which indicate sergeant's rank. The first of these has the leather gaiters worn by mountain troops; others wear the ordinary trousers with the integral gaiter which fastened around the ankle with two buttons.

▲61 ▼62

▼63

61. A purported 'combat' photograph showing Austrian infantry in action in Galicia, firing from hastily dug rifle-pits. Note the hide knapsack with the grey, rolled greatcoat strapped across the top and down each side; the standard infantry weapon was the 1895-pattern 8mm Mannlicher rifle. A variation on this equipment was used by the alpine (*Landesschützen*) units, who carried a rucksack instead of the ordinary knapsack, wore pantaloons and knee-length grey woollen stockings and carried the 1895 8mm carbine, shorter and more handy than the long infantry rifle.

62. An Austrian encampment in the Carpathians, showing typical winter dress; the central figure in the foreground wears the kepi with flap lowered to produce a Balaclava-style helmet, and the ordinary pike-grey trousers with integral gaiters fastened around the ankle with two buttons. Others have the light-grey knitted woollen cap worn in winter.

63. Serbian artillery entrained for the front line. The Serbian Army was issued with a greenish-grey service uniform from 1912, but only front-line troops received it; others wore old coloured uniforms or even civilian clothing. The uniform comprised a single-breasted tunic with breast- and side-pockets, loose trousers (tight on the lower leg), low boots and double-breasted greatcoat, with facing-coloured collar-patches (black for artillery, as here, crimson for infantry), and the head-dress was a plain cloth cap. Officers wore facing-coloured velvet collars, a peaked kepi, and riding-boots or leather gaiters and ankle-boots. The standard weapon was the 1893 7.65mm Mauser rifle.

64. A German transport-wagon stuck on the eastern front; as one dispatch stated, 'The mud of Poland is a national asset. . . . At the present moment it is fighting, silently but none the less effectively, on the side of the Allies.' The soldiers are members of the German 'train' corps, wearing the 1910 tunic with 'Swedish' cuffs, and the peaked cap worn by transport, medical and ordnance personnel, with a light-blue band and piping for train battalions (black band and red piping for motor-transport).

65. The shako was worn by the German *Jäger* and *Schützen* (rifle) units, the machine-gun battalions, signal units, the *Landwehr* (second-line infantry of which 96 regiments existed in 1914) and by the *Landsturm*, the home-defence units which frequently had outdated equipment. Like the *Pickelhaube*, the shako had a fabric cover for active service, usually grey-green, often with an Iron Cross badge, the distinctive insignia of the *Landwehr* from its inception in 1813; and an oval cockade. This *Landwehr* soldier is equipped for winter on the eastern front, with a rabbit-skin coat over his greatcoat.

64 ▲

66. German infantry on the eastern front, wearing white coats (with fur on the inside), which served for both warmth and camouflage. Both wear the field-grey field cap (*Mütze*) with two cockades, the imperial

black/white/red at the top and the state cockade on the band. This band was red for most infantry, black for rifles and artillery, light-green for *Jäger* and Bavarian machine-gun battalions, blue for medical

officers and officials and light-blue for transport units; on active service the coloured band was sometimes covered by a strip of field-grey cloth.

65 ▼

66 ▼

▲67

67. Russian Maxim gun screened by foliage. The crew wear summer service uniform, with the rolled greatcoat slung bandolier-fashion, with the aluminium mess-tin fitted on to the end of the roll. At the left side was carried a waterproof

▼69

canvas haversack containing the spare clothing and equipment, and from the rear of the waist-belt the 'Linneman tool', a small entrenching-spade.

68. The winter uniform of the Russian Army: a grey-brown

astrakhan cap with a flap which could be lowered to cover the ears and neck, and bearing a cockade as on the field-cap; and the grey-brown greatcoat (*Shinel*) with falling collar, which fastened with hooks and eyes. The bandolier is one-sixth

▲68

of a shelter-tent, folded with the greatcoat when the latter was rolled over the shoulder. The photograph shows Gabriel Elchain, a French volunteer who enrolled in a Siberian regiment, speaking to a member of a Petrograd city delegation.

69. Siberian infantry in the streets of Warsaw, wearing winter campaign uniform of astrakhan cap and greatcoat; by unfastening a half-belt at the rear of the coat, it could be used as a blanket or cloak. Over the haversacks can be seen the water-canteen (aluminium or the older, copper version); some wear the greatcoat-skirts turned back off the legs, in French fashion.

70. The Russian advance-guard in Galicia: infantry in the streets of Kielce, Poland. The second dismounted man from the left has a furled marker-flag attached to his bayonet: battalion flags had black, orange and white horizontal stripes with the battalion number on the central stripe. Company flags were red, blue, white or dark-green according to whether the regiment was the 1st, 2nd, 3rd or 4th of its division (colours matching the regimental greatcoat collar-patches), with horizontal and vertical stripes indicating the company or battalion. The duck is perhaps a regimental mascot.

71. A Russian field-battery in action, supposedly near Przemysl. The artillery wore the khaki shirt and trousers, with their red arm-of-service colour borne on the shoulder-straps and as piping to the black greatcoat-patches. The shoulder-straps bore a stencilled crossed cannon device and brigade number in Roman numerals. To the rear of the gun in the foreground are piled the crew's greatcoat-bandoliers.

70▲

71▼

▲72

72. Russian artillery in Poland, wearing winter campaign dress of greatcoat and astrakhan cap. The officer (with binoculars, second right) carries his sabre in the peculiarly Russian fashion, the hilt pointing towards the rear.

▼74

73. The most exotic Russian units were the Caucasian cossacks, who wore a grey astrakhan cap and kaftan, the Terek *voisko* (territorial division) having blue shoulder-straps and greatcoat collar-patches and the Kuban *voisko*

red. The largest cossack group, however, was the *Stepnoy* (Steppe) Cossacks, who wore ordinary uniform (as here), with the facing-colour of the *voisko* on their shoulder-straps, greatcoat-patches and as stripes on their blue trousers (khaki

▲73

trousers were introduced later). Exceptions were the Don cossacks (red distinctive, but blue shoulder-straps piped red), Amur (green distinctive, but yellow shoulder-strap piping and trouser-stripes) and Cossack artillery (red shoulder-straps, black collar-patch piped red). Shoulder-straps for all rank-and-file were khaki with light-blue numbers or badges, dark-blue for artillery.

74. The Indian Corps of the Meerut and Lahore Divisions began landing in France in late September 1914. Among the finest of these troops, the officers of the 1st Battalion, Garwhal Rifles are shown in this most significant photograph. Sailing immediately from India, they were not equipped for European service: the light colour of the khaki drill

uniform (with shorts!) contrasts greatly with the khaki serge of the second lieutenant at the extreme right, and a tropical helmet is even visible inside the tent! Seated right is the battalion's French interpreter, wearing the 'INT' brassard.

75. A Maxim-gun section of the Indian Corps advances at the double, apparently in the vicinity of Lille. The Maxim with tripod had to be carried in this manner; the men wear a roll at the rear in the manner of the British 1903-pattern bandolier equipment. The men at the rear carry boxes of ammunition.

76. Indian cavalry on the march near the Franco-Belgian border, armed with lances and wrapped-up in greatcoats, the weather being quite the opposite of that experienced on leaving India.

The Lahore Division's cavalry was the 15th Lancers (Cureton's Multanis) and the Meerut Division's the 4th Cavalry. The 20th Deccan Horse, 34th Prince Albert Victor's Own Poona Horse and the Jodhpur Imperial Service Lancers formed (with the 7th Dragoon Guards) the attached Secunderabad Cavalry Brigade.

▲79

77. The first trenches to be constructed were generally very different from the more sophisticated type which became familiar later in the war; this is a typical communication-trench filled with British 'Tommies', impossibly narrow and of very limited defensive value.

78. First Ypres: a corporal (rear), second lieutenant (right) and company sergeant-major, 1st Battalion Cameronians (Scottish Rifles) observing from a primitive trench. Officers of Scottish regiments had 'gauntlet' cuffs on their tunic, with the same system of rank-badges as the others: here, the single star of second lieutenants. The crown over three chevrons badge of the NCO indicated company sergeant-major and company quartermaster-sergeant until 1915. The officer retains the unique rifle-green regimental glengarry with black tape

▲77   ▼78

80▲

edging, tuft and ribbons; the others have knitted 'cap-comforters'.

79. A defensive trench on the front line along the Aisne, held by the Essex Regiment. Captain Maitland of the Essex faces the camera; the officer with binoculars is a FOO (Forward Observation Officer) of the Royal Artillery. Along the trench in the background can be seen the rifles of the defenders, lying in readiness across the parapet.

80. Mud was a universal problem from the earliest days of trench warfare. In this picture from late 1914, British troops are using an improvised ladle to scoop out mud from the bottom of their trench. They wear typical winter service dress, the khaki single-breasted greatcoat with deep folding collar, knitted mufflers and caps, with the ordinary web equipment worn over the greatcoat.

81. British infantry rifle-inspection in late 1914, showing a selection of typical campaign uniforms, the men having removed their equipment. Only the lance-corporal (left) appears to wear the correct uniform; others have no puttees but apparently long stockings pulled up to the knee. The second lieutenant, examining the barrel of the lance-corporal's Lee-Enfield, wears the usual cord breeches but a very unmilitary

pair of gum-boots, a common expedient in the trenches.

82. Cuisine in the trenches: British infantrymen cook a meal in late 1914. All wear the standard khaki greatcoat, knitted mufflers and Balaclava helmets. The kidney-shaped mess-tin could be used as a cooking-vessel as well as a plate. Note the knife tucked into the puttee of the man at the left.

81▼

82▼

▲83

83. In the winter of 1914 a most unusual garment was issued to the British Expeditionary Force: goatskin coats and jerkins to combat the cold weather. Nicknamed 'Teddy Bears' by the British troops, the garments came in all colours and designs, which may be observed from this company parade just behind the front line in late November or early December 1914.

▼84

84. Improvisation in the trenches: French troops prepare to launch a grenade by means of a crude catapult. Such items were used in considerable numbers: the 'firer' wears the kepi with blue-grey service cover, while the 'loader' has the 1897-pattern fore-and-aft *bonnet de police* (forage-cap) in blue-grey cloth.

85. Typical 'trench uniform': Lieutenant Bruce Bairnsfather, 1st Battalion Royal Warwickshire Regiment, at St-Yvon on Christmas Day 1914, on his way to join the 'Christmas truce' between British and German front-line troops. Later made famous by his brilliant cartoons, Bairnsfather wears a sheepskin coat, Balaclava helmet and gum-boots. Behind him is a flooded hole made by a 'Jack Johnson' shell.

86. German infantry at the firestep of a sandbagged trench. The officer (right) wears the ordinary tunic (with rank indicated by the design and number of stars on the laced shoulder-straps), and the NCOs and officers' version of the field cap, which had a peak; the side-pockets of the tunic are clearly visible. Suspended from the private's bayonet-scabbard is the *Troddel* or knot, the colouring of which identified the company and battalion. The basic infantry weapon was the 7.9mm Mauser *Gewehr* '98 with 5-round magazine; 20-round magazines were used to increase the rate of fire but made the weapon more cumbersome to use.

87. Civilian transport was commandeered by all armies, but this vehicle in German service is unusual: a London omnibus, originally used to transport British troops, but captured in Belgium by the Germans. The infantrymen in front are identified by their helmet-numerals as belonging to the 87th (1st Nassau) Regiment of XVIII Corps, of Albrecht of Württemberg's Fourth Army. They wear the 1910 *Waffenrock* and have the old (1895-pattern) ammunition-pouches on the waist-belt, worn with its usual shoulder-braces.

85 ▲   86 ▲   87 ▼

▲88

88. Newly invented armoured cars were operated by British and Belgian crews and fought many skirmishing actions against the German advance patrols along the Belgian frontier, the terrain being ideally suited to fast-moving motorized units, though mechanization was met with resistance from the more entrenched traditionalists. This vehicle was operated by the Royal Naval Air Service under Flight-Commander Samson, RN, and was crewed by a

mixture of naval and Royal Marine personnel, under the aegis of the Royal Flying Corps. Its sides were protected by steel plates, and it had a Maxim gun mounted on the 'conning tower'.

89. Flying uniform was entirely at the discretion of the individual aviator, though that depicted here is typical, worn by Flight-Sergeant William H. Duckworth of the Royal Flying Corps: a waterproof raincoat with fur lining, fur-lined leather

helmet, and apparently boots with high leather gaiters.

90. Military aviation was in its infancy in 1914, but most of the combatant nations had some type of airborne reconnaissance facility. Here Belgian aviators sit by their machine; note the wing service cap; and ordinary trousers and puttees. The woven insignia on the left sleeve of the capless officer, whose laced kepi lies on the ground beside him.

91. British aviation personnel

▲89

wore a unique uniform; although officers often retained the uniform and insignia of their original regiments, enlisted members of the Royal Flying Corps wore a khaki lancer-style 'maternity jacket' with side pockets, and which fastened down the right breast, and the 'Austrian'-pattern field-cloth shoulder-title (white on dark-blue or black) read

▼90

▼91

92▲ 93▼

'ROYAL/FLYING CORPS' or, as in this photograph of Private George Steer, the initials 'RFC'.

92. Although most military operations in 1914 occurred in Europe, minor expeditions were undertaken against German colonies. Operations against the German territory of Cameroon began as early as September 1914, from the British base at Freetown, Sierra Leone. This photograph shows a British West African contingent embarking at Freetown to attack the German port of Duala, the point of entry to Cameroon on the Bight of Biafra. Despite the workmanlike uniform of 'shirt-sleeves', shorts and topee, it is interesting to note that the officer at left retains a sword suspended from his Sam Browne belt.

93. Japanese participation in the war against the Central Powers was restricted to maritime operations and one military expedition, against the German Chinese colony of Tsingtau, the 'Gibraltar of the Far East', in late 1914. In collaboration with a British-Indian contingent, the Japanese Expeditionary Force captured

Tsingtau on 7 November 1914. These Japanese infantry are eating a hasty meal a short distance from the firing-line; they wear European-style uniform peaked cap and heavy greatcoats. Note the 'rising sun' banner in the centre.

94. A scene which was to be repeated countless times from 1914 onward: men of the Loyal Regiment (North Lancashire) pay brief homage to the temporary graves of their comrades, winter 1914. The Loyals formed part of the 2nd

Infantry Brigade of I Corps, and are shown here in greatcoats with the 1908 web equipment (less knapsack) worn over the top. Note the shaft of the entrenching-tool carried on the bayonet-scabbard.

94▼

The *Fotofax* series

A new range of pictorial studies of military subjects for the modeller, historian and enthusiast. Each title features a carefully-selected set of photographs plus a data section of facts and figures on the topic covered. With line drawings and detailed captioning, every volume represents a succinct and valuable study of the subject. New and forthcoming titles:

Warbirds
F-111 Aardvark
P-47 Thunderbolt
B-52 Stratofortress
Stuka!
Jaguar
US Strategic Air Power:
  Europe 1942–1945
Dornier Bombers
RAF in Germany

Vintage Aircraft
German Naval Air Service
Sopwith Camel
Fleet Air Arm, 1920–1939
German Bombers of WWI

Soldiers
World War One: 1914
World War One: 1915
World War One: 1916
Union Forces of the American
  Civil War
Confederate Forces of the
  American Civil War
Luftwaffe Uniforms
British Battledress 1945–1967
  (2 vols)

Warships
Japanese Battleships, 1897–
1945
Escort Carriers of World War
  Two
German Battleships, 1897–
1945
Soviet Navy at War, 1941–1945
US Navy in World War Two,
1943–1944
US Navy, 1946–1980 (2 vols)
British Submarines of World
  War One

Military Vehicles
The Chieftain Tank
Soviet Mechanized Firepower
  Today
British Armoured Cars since
1945
NATO Armoured Fighting
  Vehicles
The Road to Berlin
NATO Support Vehicles

The *Illustrated* series

The internationally successful range of photo albums devoted to current, recent and historic topics, compiled by leading authors and representing the best means of obtaining your own photo archive.

Warbirds
US Spyplanes
USAF Today
Strategic Bombers, 1945–1985
Air War over Germany
Mirage
US Naval and Marine Aircraft
  Today
USAAF in World War Two
B-17 Flying Fortress
Tornado
Junkers Bombers of World War
  Two
Argentine Air Forces in the
  Falklands Conflict
F-4 Phantom Vol II
Army Gunships in Vietnam
Soviet Air Power Today
F-105 Thunderchief
Fifty Classic Warbirds
Canberra and B-57
German Jets of World War Two

Vintage Warbirds
The Royal Flying Corps in
  World War One
German Army Air Service in
  World War One
RAF between the Wars
The Bristol Fighter
Fokker Fighters of World War
  One
Air War over Britain, 1914–
1918
Nieuport Aircraft of World War
  One

Tanks
Israeli Tanks and Combat
  Vehicles
Operation Barbarossa
Afrika Korps
Self-Propelled Howitzers
British Army Combat Vehicles
  1945 to the Present
The Churchill Tank
US Mechanized Firepower
  Today
Hitler's Panzers
Panzer Armee Afrika
US Marine Tanks in World War
  Two

Warships
The Royal Navy in 1980s
The US Navy Today
NATO Navies of the 1980s
British Destroyers in World
  War Two
Nuclear Powered Submarines
Soviet Navy Today
British Destroyers in World
  War One
The World's Aircraft Carriers,
  1914–1945
The Russian Convoys, 1941–
1945
The US Navy in World War
  Two
British Submarines in World
  War Two
British Cruisers in World War
  One
U-Boats of World War Two
Malta Convoys, 1940–1943

Uniforms
US Special Forces of World
  War Two
US Special Forces 1945 to the
  Present
The British Army in Northern
  Ireland
Israeli Defence Forces, 1948 to
  the Present
British Special Forces, 1945 to
  Present
US Army Uniforms Europe,
  1944–1945
The French Foreign Legion
Modern American Soldier
Israeli Elite Units
US Airborne Forces of World
  War Two
The Boer War
The Commandos World War
  Two to the Present
Victorian Colonial Wars

A catalogue listing these series and other Arms & Armour Press titles is available on request from: Sales Department, Arms & Armour Press, Artillery House, Artillery Row, London SW1P 1RT.